Contents

 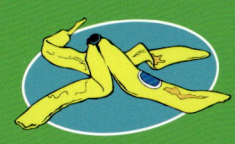

Safety

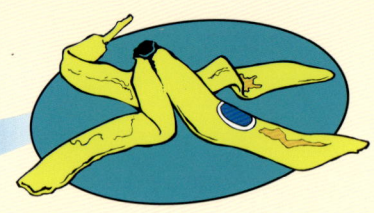

BE PREPARED!

Your baby will start to move, grab anything lying around and put it into his or her mouth!

- Keep small things like coins and buttons well out of reach to avoid choking.

- Put tablecloths away; one tug and your baby could be scalded by hot food or drinks.

- Move sharp objects, glasses and other breakable items well out of reach.

- Keep plants out of reach.

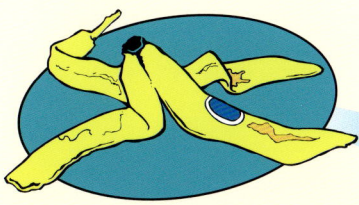

● Always use a fireguard for all heaters and fires.

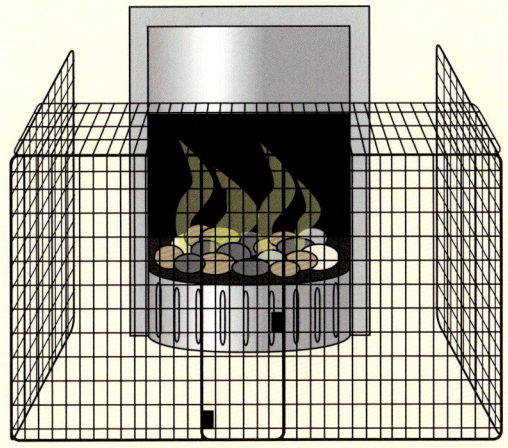

● Stairs should be blocked with safety gates at the top and the bottom of the stairs.

5

Safety

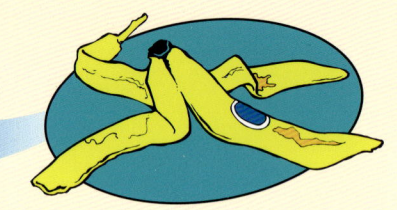

- Never leave an iron unattended.

- Keep all cleaning products and medicines out of reach, in a locked cupboard.

● Water from the hot tap can scald. Always run the cold water before the hot and don't leave the hot tap running.

● NEVER leave babies and small children alone in the bath. They can drown in just a few centimetres of water.

Safety

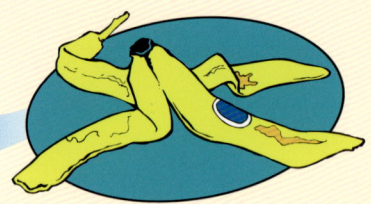

- It is safest for babies to travel in rear-facing car seats. They should only be transferred to a forward-facing car seat when they are able to sit up on their own.
Put rear-facing car seats in the back seat of the car.

REMEMBER - NEVER USE A REAR-FACING CAR SEAT IN THE FRONT OF A CAR WITH A PASSENGER AIRBAG.

● BABYSITTING

Your baby should only be left with a responsible adult.

Children under 14 should not be left to care for babies and young children.

● Never leave your baby in the house alone, even if they are sleeping.

Home Alone

Healthy Eating

● Start to introduce your baby to solid foods from 6 months. Begin with small quantities of pureed fruit or vegetables, or baby rice that can be made up with breast or formula milk. Try these either before, during or after the usual milk feed.

Gradually increase the amount of solid food offered.

● Foods should be offered on a shallow plastic spoon, never from a bottle.

● When preparing baby's food all utensils must be clean and all plastic feeding equipment should be sterilized first.

Healthy Eating

● Never add extra salt or sugar to baby's food.

Sugar encourages a sweet tooth and leads to tooth decay.

Salt is harmful to babies.

● Give your baby a variety of foods with different tastes, but avoid very spicy or fried foods.

● Offer savoury foods. Sweets and chocolates are not good for baby.

● Pasteurised cows' milk (silver top) can only be introduced from 12 months.

Healthy Eating

- Do not keep opened tins or jars of baby food for longer than 24 hours; remember to empty the remaining food into a clean dish and keep it covered in the fridge.

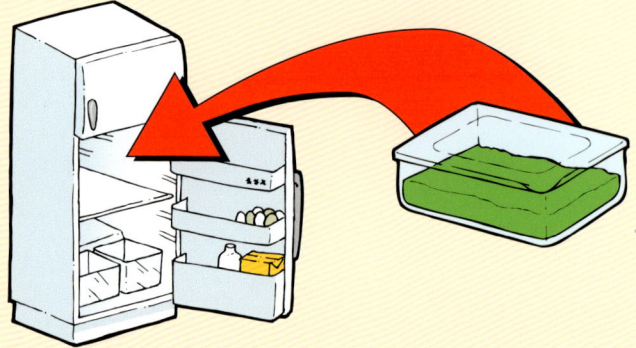

- Only heat enough food for one meal at a time.

- Never reheat food that baby has not eaten.

Healthy Eating

- In the highchair,
  fit a safety harness and
  always use it.

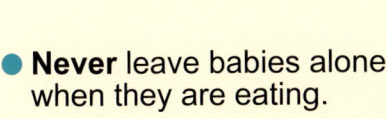

- **Never** leave babies alone
  when they are eating.

Oral Hygiene

- Give cool boiled water to drink between meals.

- Encourage your baby to drink from a cup as soon as he or she can hold one, but do not use an anti-drip beaker.

NO! YES!

Oral Hygiene

● Sweetened drinks lead to tooth decay.
Do not give drinks containing sugar to your baby.

Glucose, glucose syrup, fructose, concentrated fruit juice, sucrose, dextrose, honey, invert sugar, maltose, hydrolysed starch.

● These are alternative names for sugars. They can harm your baby's developing teeth.

Oral Hygiene

- Dummies are useful to settle babies in their younger weeks, but should not be used excessively for older babies.

- Limit dummies to going to sleep times, only remove when baby is asleep.

- Try to get rid of all dummies and bottles by the time your child reaches their first birthday.

Oral Hygiene

- As soon as your baby's first tooth appears you need a baby toothbrush and child's toothpaste to brush twice a day.

PM

AM

- Register your baby with a dentist.

Keeping Active

Your baby will now be starting to crawl and pull himself or herself up using the furniture.

- Make sure that your baby gets time and space to crawl and explore his environment with you watching close by.

- Make time for a walk every day – great exercise for Mum and good for baby too.

And don't forget even a newborn baby needs strapping into a buggy with a harness.

18

Keeping Active

- Do not use baby walkers - research shows that they do not teach children to walk. Baby walkers can tip over very easily causing accidents.

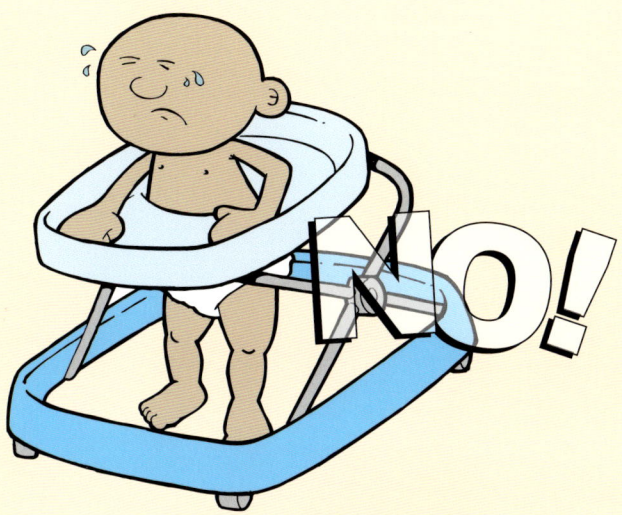

- Young babies do not need shoes until they are walking.

Keeping Active

- Take time to enjoy the great outdoors.

Fun in the Sun

Never leave your baby in direct sunlight. Young children have sensitive skin that needs to be protected.

- Find shade
- Cover up
- Apply a high factor sun screen
- Provide extra, cool drinks.

Keeping Active

- Swimming is great exercise for baby and for Mum and Dad too.
Contact your local pool for details of special 'Water Babies' sessions.

- Keep Fit sessions are a great way to keep you in shape.

Early Learning

It's never too early to start playing with your baby. The best way to do this is by talking to your baby.

DO

- Tell baby what you are doing.

Mummy's just hanging up the washing.

PEEKABOO!

- Play hiding games.

DO

- Sing action songs and nursery rhymes to help your baby's developing language skills.

- Make it easier for baby to listen to you by turning off the TV and radio.

Early Learning

DO

- Listen carefully and talk back when your baby makes noises.

- Share books.

- Join your local library - they have wonderful books for babies and toddlers and don't mind how noisy or excited their young visitors get.

DO

- Have fun making sounds together

- Find out if there is a 'Toy Library' in your area for access to lots of stimulating toys to enjoy with your baby.

Contacts

In case of an **accident, emergency** or just **advice** these are some useful numbers to ring for information and help.

NHS Direct 0845 4647

Your call will automatically be put through to your nearest centre and will be charged at local rates (may be more from a mobile).
www.nhsdirect.nhs.uk

Your local Health Visitor can be contacted via your GP practice.

Add your GP's phone number here

Your local Fire Service can be contacted for advice on fire prevention

Child Accident Prevention Trust (CAPT) 020 7608 3828
A charity committed to reducing childhood injury.
www.capt.org.uk

First Aid Courses
British Red Cross 0845 608 6888
St John Ambulance 0870 010 4950

Useful numbers in your area: